HOW WE LIGHT

HOW WE LIGHT

Nick Sturm

www.h-ngm-nbks.com

FIRST H_NGM_N EDITION, 2013

ISBN 978-0-9882287-2-6

Cover by Ryan Spooner
Book design by Nate Slawson

For a complete listing of titles, or for more on this book, visit:

www.h-ngm-nbks.com
www.h-ngm-n.com/light

CONTENTS

HOW WE LIGHT

A BASIC GUIDE TO AUTOBIOGRAPHY

1. There is a lot of room in my mouth.
2. I want to put up some wallpaper and do a little singing.
3. I want it to buffalo glow.
4. I understand the confusion.
5. That's how we looked in the prisonless distance.
6. With deer in the snow like beautiful triggers.
7. Little to no time will be spent considering the role of heavy weaponry.
8. I love some people.
9. I have tried to love some people.
10. I have tried to not love some people.
11. I cried, in the restaurant, with the war, and the waitress.
12. Sometimes I feel so close to strawberries.
13. Then it's gone.
14. Then it's not.
15. Driving alone is often an occasion to contemplate freedom.
16. While weeping.
17. With our tourniquets kissing.
18. It was like the sunflower growing on the overpass between indeterminate midwestern towns, the sky a luxurious, cardinal mass, the sky a burning car calling us forward toward our own improbable portraits.
19. On Sundays I feel most in debt.
20. Don't lick that.
21. Too much cake to feel comfortable.
22. I would like to do more with chainsaws.
23. I would like to do a lot more with chainsaws.
24. I've got a few questions.
25. Where is my mother?
26. Why am I hanging from this traffic light?
27. Why am I lying?
28. Why else build a fence than to name what's on your side of

the fence The Land of Too Damn Beautiful For Anyone To Die?

29. We bought pencils and sat on milk crates and gave our feelings vague, mythic titles.
30. This made us who we were, and happy, when we could.
31. Text me snow.
32. Text me Tuesday.
33. Text me the Constitution of Finland.
34. A Basic Guide to Suffering.
35. "I want to fall asleep with you inside of me," she whispers, acknowledging how close we are to passing right through each other.
36. I only vote out of guilt.
37. I'm not going to pay for this.
38. My greatest regret: the owl still warm in the grocery bag.
39. When I was in love.
40. Don't talk to me.
41. It was summer. It was nowhere, everyone knew, and at the beaches I saw the dissolving edges, how the wound was built into me, that fantastic static particular to this latitude where the windows are always open and I, on the verge of edifying some clumpier dark, heap this arsenal. Some nights I wrote twenty page letters to friends who, as the years coiled, became trellises to a younger sense of wonder, bottles of cherry wine on the windowsill, across the harbor the bells, though that's not where they are, or I am, who you are, and the transfer point is densest in that breed of confusion.
42. I am full of bones.
43. I am ferocious and want to share.
44. I am going to keep laughing until something gores me.
45. Solution: admit that anything is a dance floor.
46. Experts say this is where I should /
47. A good thing to do would be to have fun.
48. New new new new new new sincerity.
49. After I threw the parts out the window it was easier to use them as I saw fit.

50. Consider the streets of Bruges.
51. Am I sleeping?
52. Am I skiing?
53. I can't feel my fingers.
54. You might want to close the blinds for this.
55. I'm a big fan.
56. My name is Nick and I'll be taking your order.
57. Sartre, *The Imaginary*: "[Y]ou will not necessarily grasp at a glance the sense of each line, but you will in any case know of each one that it is representative, that it stands for something and that this is the very reason for its existence."
58. In Sweden the red balloon the red balloon.
59. We're using the same technology.
60. So how come you don't believe me?
61. Solution: dream about grapes.
62. The sun is trying to kill me.
63. It's doing a wonderful job.
64. All we had for breakfast was avocado salad.
65. "How necessary you are to me and how precious."
    — Robert Desnos
66. But I still didn't have any potholders.
67. That's my coat.
68. No, the rules are not clear.
69. Even if it's a disaster, could you have imagined seeing so many phonographs?
70. Let's drink kombucha in Elk City, Oklahoma.
71. Let's do something incredible on a bluff and write a poem called "Something Incredible on a Bluff."
72. "I shall bed thee down in star-manure." — Kenneth Patchen
73. I was not wrong in the gazebo. I was only wrong.
74. What I learned at school.
75. What I learned in the rain.
76. What I learned with my tongue.
77. I went to the store to be around other people and came home with a stone swan in the passenger seat.

78. In Paris I fed a one-footed pigeon olives. I had an incredible headache.
79. The years rattled like pipes with angels inside.
80. Sartre, *The Imaginary*: "But the dream world is not so closed that the dreamer does not come to play a role in it."
81. Sartre, *The Imaginary*: "It is simply necessary that the imagery of the dreamer produces an unspecified object that the dreamer can believe, whether immediately or after some time, is themselves, whatever else that object may be."
82. Once, I was a waterfall.
83. I don't make anything up.
84. Once, I was a waterfall.
85. I have tried to live in such a way so that it is not unreasonable to travel halfway around the world only to stand in a small, silent store surrounded by unaverage violins, though I know nothing about violins, or so I thought.
86. All movements are immediate assessments of speed and direction.
87. Panda panda jugular panda.
88. The mutilated bicycles of Montgomery Street.
89. My internal instruments are not in agreement.
90. With recklessness in my nonethelesses.
91. With the vast caress of static in my head's pebbled garb.
92. With my Dixie cup full of dreams.
93. Most of it will go in the trash.
94. Standing in the sun is its own syntax.
95. I wonder what will be important tomorrow.
96. Your quiet, red shoulders.
97. Mary, can you see that small hot dog container floating in the waves like a boat?
98. It is difficult to be fatal amongst cupcakes.
99. Here is a cupcake.
100. The hummingbird in my heart says hello.

We awaken in Zurich! We go out for emotions and sodas! It is not correct
To stay anywhere for too long. Shall we go to the Moscow of flowers?
I don't know. Perhaps, but we play tennis well enough and in Albuquerque
It is too easy to lose one's jacket. Then a cloud collapsed on Brussels' silly face.
The Ferris wheel was frightening enough. In New York the conversation
Disappeared into a pack of cigarettes and would not smile. The trees of Copenhagen
And the trampolines of Houston! Swans! Photic machines! The sky stops
For a moment to take a leak. Dear Reykjavik, trying to make sense of this
Unseemly sequence makes my roses hurt. Children in Tripoli ask us insensible questions
Because we are not angels, though we cry like angels, and in San Francisco, for once,
The world opened its heart and we removed the shrapnel. After that, Stockholm
Got us drunk and taught us to dance. We shared a sandwich in Delhi
But that was only the beginning. In Frankfurt, as chance had it, we did nothing of interest.
Cleveland, I stagger through your streets like "I am trying to get as far away from this
As I can." We arrived late in Paris where we had headaches and sex and oranges. (How
Arbitrary! I feel like a cupcake!) What is the plan? What do you mean "genuine"?
Let's rent an apartment in Helsinki and sell lemonade to beautiful girls!
Let's read Swedenborg and ride jet-skis under the bridges of Amsterdam!
At the last second we are invited to a house party in Chicago where we learn
It is not possible to pour an entire bottle of wine into a violin. It's true, in Melbourne

We made terrific asses of ourselves! Sao Paulo was hot! We liked it very much!

In Bruges our souls became great works of art as we fell asleep on the grass.

In Hong Kong we spoke into the ear of oblivion and wept in golden chairs. Tulips

Grew in the gutters of Beirut. We drank coffee and believed everything was worth saying

At least once, like in Jerusalem when the girl said, "Have you ever played tennis

In Albuquerque? You look so familiar!" or when we met an old man

By the pinball machines of Guadalajara who said, "I am the owner of a red car

In the future. In Auckland I discovered a cup of tea," and we laughed at him

And asked him to add some lines to this poem (he wrote the ones about Frankfurt,

Sao Paulo, and Brussels, and might have written the one for Reykjavik, but no one

Is quite certain or cares). Oh sweet St. Petersburg where I eat tomatoes and create

Inexplicable machines in praise of accidents and laughter! In Dakar we sell cantaloupe

And are not sarcastic! We are unemotional in Istanbul! We open the dictionary

Rescuing flowers in Denver and suddenly we are starring at ourselves.

Oh never-ending stream of amusements! My zipper is broken! A kiss in Winnipeg!

WHAT A TREMENDOUS TIME WE'RE HAVING!

In many ways I am not a rabbit
or a spool of ribbon & that is important
because it is amazing How wrong
it would be to say *I am going skiing*
or *Do you want to share this cantaloupe*
when you mean *Let's do something*
incredible It is not about being specific
It is about opening up your genius mouth
& decorating what comes out in all
sorts of felt & vapor & astonishment
My friends know this & are always unlocking
the garden where I sit in my naked wreckage
I have hidden an amp in the hawthorn
There is a jackhammer in the begonias
You can use it anytime you like

A WHORL THAT ASCENDS

My hands do not think   They get
lit up   The air just happy
something is happening   A feeling
I can get my hands into   Maybe make
some noise or attract your attention
using a foam finger   A large finger
I swing mercilessly   Overhead
there are a lot of extra heads
belonging to birds   Also
someone   I am not sure
if there is a better way to say this
Someone looking at the cloud tops
from above   Like what is a law
& how can I repeat this
using words   At the exhibit I touch
everything with my mouth   My mouth
does not attract much attention   It acts
so unsure not of itself
but of the world   The world
the shape of these colors   What
an exhibit this is   What a way
to believe in this world & its clouds
All open & a whorl   My hands
when I land dressed in light   Where
I land   like my mouth
is not up to me

WHAT A TREMENDOUS TIME WE'RE HAVING!

Take off that ridiculous hat & tell me you love me
is what I want to say but my tongue is not so evolved
My tongue rides a hobbyhorse in a big wet parlor
It acts like a baby in a castle dragging one miraculous oar
& while you get smaller & smaller on the lip of the ocean
stuffing sand dollars in your fanny pack all I can do
is push my stupid tongue back into its stupid airport
& lay down in the tide where all the little crabs
take apart my teeth the way their parents taught them
& their parents before them & their parents before them
& their parents before them & their parents before them
which is when the world was the size of a gazebo
with one undying heart at the center of our lives

A BASIC GUIDE TO HISTORY

The people put everything they had into the machine patio furniture bleach symphonies the people needed a story that's why they built the machine the machine ate the blessings of the people and infected them and divided them into quadrants one quadrant was called The Island of Vague Agendas another was called The Bureau of Choreographed Screaming and another was called The Central Intelligence Agency the people did not understand how the machine distinguished between blessings or how it generated quadrants but it appeared logical and moral and such appearances were important to the people some people opposed the story generated by the machine but the discourse of the machine made the people numb and at night their fingerprints would burn and itch and so they ceased speaking of the machine on and on it went the people feeding the machine magnolia trees and foreclosed houses and the proletariat and the machine dragging the torso of experience through its thresher infecting it manipulating it into quadrants deleting as it wished once some people filmed the machine and when they watched the tape they saw that the machine was transparent that they could see inside of it and this made the machine obsolete the machine was not real the people were real the people with the symphonies and patio furniture people began looking in the mirror and seeing themselves people drank water out of drinking fountains and felt it inside their throats people hung signs that said we are

governed by nothing we are governed by nothing
but light

THE KIDS ARE STILL GROWING

I awoke surrounded
by glowing   Tall grass
brushing against my wrists
My dad was there & my mom
was there   They looked
specifically plover
I said   A cloud is a kind of
heavy machinery   I said
Hear me out   A platypus
is not an elaborate hoax
The mechanics of light
are unimaginable   I was
full of these things   These
things were coming out
like people from airplanes   I
had arrived & arriving was like
a small sleeping   Suddenly
my wingspan was incredible
Suddenly the door was
drifting   Geometry
tuning itself   I said some
more things   I said my mask
is a thousand roses   I was
a red shipwreck carrying balloons
I said   My party dress
is in the style of the late queen
My front legs are tenacious   I said
There is a perceivable whine
in my child bones   My dad was
glowing too   He said   We have to
modify our coffee program
My glowing mom said   I'm going

to Italy   These things seemed
important   But why was
I here   Why did I have all these
things inside me with no river
to put them in   It was just me
with all these new things   Not
alone but kind of   Every night
mauling myself to sleep

A BASIC GUIDE TO EMERGENCY

There were rooms built with thorns. Lovers were screaming
it into their pillows. It was flowers doing awful things to the sky.
It was a cop with binoculars down your throat. Your throat
that was sleeping in the wolf. Your throat that was saturated
with snow. Throat pruning its own meat. Throat eating its last
mirror. Multiplicity and rot. Birth and holy shock. Throat of split
sense without gauge without die without amount with outbreak
and the rage of the voice tethered to its own chemical grammar.
What if it were your father? Would it matter who was watching?
It was a blossom of the it in its own shatter and crease. An attack
in the diamond. A diamond in the ugly pain. The pain that ate
us and was embryonic and starling and was stored inside us
like a melted carnival ride. Art recorded it. Art made it laugh
electric and accident. Art killed history and went to the aquarium.
Art of the fuckup. Art of the hoard. Diesel art. Art that you dig
out of the tongue on a rainy day and cry and cry and why
is this body such fragile shrapnel? Such distance and angel?
Art made the body feel grass. Art made the body feel surge
and crux. Art disassociated the body from God and left it
naked with a cell phone containing one vast number. Every
moment is an emergency and every emergency is an array
of juxtapositions and grace. We went it together in the green
ambulance having fallen from art. Together in the tangent
that led to us being together at all. Together in Oklahoma
where the streets are clogged with sky. Together and gasping.
Pressed together in the metamorphic volume. Made together
for nothing and a bowl of cherries in the tourniquet sun. What
I mean to say is I love you but it's not going to be okay.

SPORADIC RESISTANCE

It was all wrong   The radio
sobbing   The windows cursing
me & my silly ass parade of synaptic
misfires   A kind of déjà vu where you
are always almost falling into my arms
A brutal veering while the cat keeps
sleeping   But all I'm doing is
describing something I can't
& I really can't   I just want
to say   These are pretty whatever
they are   To not fight myself
replaying our joke about where my mind
is in the morning   I'm always right here
towing an anchor through the flowers
without you & I don't want to admit that
sustains me as much as it kills me   I'm not
admitting that   I'm admitting that
it's my faltering I couldn't give up   Couldn't
pick up a trumpet or your hand & remember
what else I can do with this mouth
But look at me reaching after fact & reason
when I need it least   The breeze gasps
against me   I lick my wounds
into knots   A full-size horse
walks into the middle of the room
& we ride

WHAT A TREMENDOUS TIME WE'RE HAVING!

All morning I linger in the courtyard
thawing amidst the knots of luminous weeds
I feel like an air conditioner emitting
a kind of stupid music for you but all I want
is to not be invisible In the courtyard
the sun acts like it is having a party
It is a small cathedral smeared
with intelligence I begin to ripen & know
I am a mammal lucky to have a mouth
So I will use it I open the door I step
inside & fall apart at your feet like a hand-
made piñata It is sad but also amazing
The way the light becomes drunk against
the architecture of your body The way
we use our mouths against one another

A BASIC GUIDE TO TRUTH

In Norway a child is holding a cloud.

Elephants are big and sometimes small.

Everything would be different without water.

Thank you water cycle.

Thank you dynamic natural systems.

We are friends.

Under the snow there is a green door.

You have three hearts.

One looks like a tree.

One looks like a cage full of water.

The other one looks like an elephant.

And it is very big.

And it is in Norway.

Speaking Norwegian.

Behind a door.

In the forest.

Alone.

THE ERA OF CONFUSION BEGINS

I want to be a smaller pony   I want
to be a silver cup   For the flowers to
stand up & furnish my life with joy
I don't want to be a pile of duct tape
& sun   I don't want to be a candle
burning in a tiny temple   No
I want to be some handsome
acoustic behavior   All formlessness
& you & me wet with content   The sea
overwhelming us   A big fumbling
window collecting in the sky   There's nothing
I'd rather be doing than having
elaborate hedonistic parties   Than using
my mouth to love you   But now it's just
me   Me with my pony hands burning down
to rain   The sun making noise all over
my pony face   Your face telling me
from afar there is no smaller pony

WHAT A TREMENDOUS TIME WE'RE HAVING!

I wash my laundry in blue sauce
My tribe gnaws on the radio & speaks
misguided into the ether It is not clear
what we are singing or where we are going
to store this million pounds of ice cream
I am a sphere of light hovering over a sandwich
I have a slow colorful thought
blinking in my cortex An entire history of
beautiful people falling asleep with cats
is somehow irrelevant What the hell
do we think we're celebrating
Sunflowers have the hospital surrounded
Everything I wear smells like the mountains
The part of me that is speaking is the only part
of me in the mountains

THE ROOST

It takes a little silence   Some spit
to sing   The way building
an altar of coffee & talk
stains us holy & un-   Twists us
family   My family of birdhearts
hurtling into teenage lakes   Our faces
sullen   Our asses great
& great are the flames
that lick our engines   Great are
the trees that floor us   Love us
Render us wealthy with pleasure
When the sun turns off we assemble
into palaces of beer   Into the trial
& error of this confounding
gala   You tell me to keep
my eyes on the distant bodily
softness   That we're getting closer
together   To bed down in
the inexplicable   Which
is kind of hot   Which is wet
& an actual belief system
Basically lemonade   The shared
mist on our lips   All of this is
maybe a mistake   Maybe a joke
about going to the inappropriate
woods   But either way
joy   Either joy or
more joy   All accident   Our
little religion drunk on clouds
& la la la   You know
what I mean   Birds of a feather
fuck & fuck-up together

COMMONWEALTH OF LONG BLUE FLOWERS

Amorous & haunted   Bitterness
& bells   What kind of sorrow
is only yours   One path leads
to the waterfall   The other
to the trash heap & your soul is all
busted up for either   Performing impractical
actions with impractical results   Same old
feeling obsessively rendered   Unraveling
& uncertain   Mandible & stumble
I'm not sure a hatchet would help
what you keep in your blouse   I want
to say I'm intact but my head is more
flare gun than firework   A call for help
masked in oh my god that's beautiful
Make a mess   Read a book   We all
might need to go to bed more often
together   Put on & take off our
intentions without purpose   It's all good
as long as no one's decent   As long as
we end up loose & whipped by mist
into gladness   Nothing I feel
I keep for myself   Everything I lose
I give back in flowers   Promise & principle
Riot & grace   Since I got here
I've been hugging everyone

WHAT A TREMENDOUS TIME WE'RE HAVING!

I wake up and muzzle my soul
with a kind of pale tenderness
My mouth automatically dismantles
the remarkable geometry of a tangerine
It starts to look like I don't have a choice
My password has to contain at least
one special character A billion flowers
aren't for sale anywhere in this world
A threshold sounds like it should be
some kind of magnificent art
but it is only another boundary
between my body & the spacious day
I have an overwhelming urge
to use a forklift improperly
I am not going to wear any underwear
One year ago today I planted a tree
Happy birthday Happy birthday

ACTUALS & POSSIBLES

You say a negative thing about pudding
& I simply cannot agree   We throw our hands
in the air & spend all day discovering
our newfound handlessness   It is liberating
but also frustrating to not agree   About furnishings
About windswept plains   About what to name
what we're doing   Is it debris removal
or a dream   Is it a squirrel in the sun
or a squirrel in the rain   When there is an idea
I hear it is easier to have your own idea
by saying no to the other idea   I like that
A spoon jangles in a cup & a spoon
does not jangle in a cup   One or more
things change & that is called life
O life   O pudding   Release me   Let me
sputter in the grass all morning looking
for a way in   A way into the party where
I'm told how long I've been sleeping
& I simply must agree   So I wake up
& feel

FAKE WHITE COUCH

Hello anonymous harbor   Hello
friendly people at the barbeque   I am done
sleeping   Thank you & now I would like
to hum a little   Avoid meat with you   Laugh
for specific reasons   One being that I am saying
impossible things about couches   Another being
the arc of complicated feelings   How they
cover us with mistakes   These human things
Anchors & pieces of toast   Anything to make you
empathize with me in a poncho   That's how
dumbly I feel   Compared to me even
a small boat is bigger   Always limited by shape
& a necessity for quiet people speaking loudly
about slinkies & whales   For no reason
I love them   In a dream   This ability to smuggle
our hands into each other's hair   Hello quick
suffocating sweetness   Hello somebody
with impractical wisdom about hand signals
Your shoes are great   Also the energy
we exchange   How it is carried around
for a long time   Even in the backyard   Even
in a small boat going far away   Everyone is like
wow   With shame on my heart & lemonade
in my mouth   This is my best disguise

THE FENCES

I built a fence I built a fence out of wood I built a
fence out of fence parts I built a fence out of
orange peels I built a fence out of satellite dishes
and yellow paint I built a fence out of skulls I
built a fence out of my love for you people said it
looked like it would stand forever and I wasn't
going to tell them otherwise I built a fence out of
daffodils and enchiladas and devotion to
something larger than myself that I knew I could
not grasp I built a fence out of coupons and
statues of the Virgin Mary and maps of 16th
century Holland I built a fence out of my friends
and called it The Capital of My Heart I built a
fence out of pornography and covered it in a
black sheet which made everyone look and gasp
and get very excited I built a fence lying on my
back in the dark I built a fence with my tax return
and it was the smallest fence anyone had ever
seen I built a fence out of paintings that museums
buy but don't hang in galleries because of
intellectual censorship I built a fence out of old
cell phones and baby teeth I built a fence out of
bullet casings and concrete I built a fence out of
seagulls and key chains and teacups that have
never been used I built a fence out of my
powerlessness in the face of the absolute and had
enough tears to build fences everyday for the rest
of my life I built a fence out of blackened tofu
and kale I built a fence out of pieces of fire and
dull knives I built a fence out of my past and my
pants I built a fence out of bacon and lack of
compassion and called it the Republican Party I

built a fence out of what was left after the war
nothing was left after the war but time to build
fences I built a fence out of all the ties that belong
to the President of the United States of America I
built a fence out of what was left in the apartment
after you left me and laid in the vacancy of my
bed and could smell pancakes the neighbors were
making pancakes I built a fence out of red birds
and ice and gravestones and ice machines and
gravestone machines I built a fence

HOW WE LIGHT

Dear Darkness,

Summer has been unusually long so let me just say
fuck you   this morning

                                    for the first time
my head declared an official ceasefire

I wrote a friend a letter
a smudged green feeling sitting at a window in the hidden
architecture of my wrists I felt like I was surviving this feeling

all over me in the pavilion of unsyntactical promise
        the punch you know
in your blood what I'm talking about I wrote I'm sure
you're in love with something or somebody you know
you don't love enough or maybe I wrote

you're standing on a beach somewhere holding
a peach like some kind of hero it's this way says one

human to another pretty human you are
one of the youngest things in the world we're all

dawned on our wrists on the soft
blue truce I've made with death the last thing I wrote Darkness
this is for you
                        was the first thing

I am in the morning is a pony
named Kenneth

everyday
I pass through the park eating snacks

attempting to do something fabulous hand my friend a bag
of almonds of course there is no reason not to

imagine what I'm seeing a way I'm not seeing it

earlier I washed the dishes and in the warm water
my hands were bridges full of blood good

not because of what they are but because they are
doing something   reaching across

the bed in some near and gentle future
where my friend says   we are dead
and actually just naked somewhere else
in the sound of my whole being   hearing I believe

with the muzzle of delicacy smashed against you Darkness
for as long as I can
I will know where to turn my head

to hear you fresh from sleeping

in the street how
we light is obvious

sore in the circus the sea
in me the scattering means some purring
in us awake an elaborate system I am sometimes

reduced to a spectator but I won't stay
in line only in lines I feel more
human here all this endlessness
dismembering the music in us there isn't an adequate word

for what's turning into an afternoon between us crashing us
        on account of where brightness is kept my hair smells
like mint I'll never know exactly how

            I'm supposed to feel
        exactly the breeze

is beautiful all at once and at once I desire a better
word I should have said
                        world I really wish

I could communicate something
            this unusual and lilac-like feeling you

smile inside your speaking I shouldn't need
a password for that   in the cozy urgency

of a yellow room a square
yellow room I am assured where the Darkness pushes

        against us we are letting the Darkness know
we're here on the porch the breeze feels let me
try again

like white paws like constant curtains like the ruination of politics
            if you need me Darkness

I'll be making pies all night
with my friends in the caramel harbor
of common feeling you will be asked

            wicked and full of health to please
        enjoy yourself

                who doesn't
want to kiss until morning clasping the nourishing

arc of grief letting yourself laugh at some unimportant moment
             crowded with arguments of how buoyant
or not the day is becoming

                  one continually growing maw

dedicated to the smell of rosemary
             on your palms   some vital exchange
of breath we might all allow ourselves

                  to be surrendered to beyond the wild
                       blue light below our voices this endless table

we insist upon vibrating upon and I'm not too shy to ask
                       you through every possible window if it feels good

             in this book of dreams you have permission

to lick and fail and feel raw in the ruins where at breakfast
our hearts are breeding in these bodies these vowel structures
                  these fence posts in snow the sure

need to share in the glistening
                  a thing with wings
stands up in us and begins

an uneven faith peels off me Darkness like Keats basically
I'd rather be an Eagle and when he wrote Eagle
             he capitalized Eagle as a way to believe

in the power of the nouns we are to save us I promise
                  we're going to be delivered
something more than coupons in the ceaseless
             kingdom of noise I have this feeling

of accountability I have
no idea what I deserve

my cell phone bill is due and where my love are you

I will not be a tool for bitterness over and over I admit
I have dreamt against the law of your cheek
going backwards and forwards simultaneously I want to

drape solace across the invisible sound of you
your quiet shoulders the memory

I woke up in to suffer this lack of definition
in each other's hair for a little while we forget

the government has assigned us each a secret number

so I stand alone in the yard at night
forging my mangled crime in every color

braced against exhaustion scattered everywhere
with skin I'm going
to go lay with my sovereign

dreams I want you
to touch me first
I'm tired of knowing
giving away the snow in me

let's digress into mist
build lamps out of the laughing
we give to the wound just sitting in the park
looking at swans we mostly never touch

each other other than

when we're asking to be broken
        for the future even if it makes me a shameful man
I believe in hoping towards knowing
we are thinking of each other

                where the shattered blue settles I write
the rent check and watch someone string lights
        in the trees today that's their job

the point being to generate
        a larger feeling

not visibly located but diffused
                in every layer I am
        one unfolding sequin a glaring piece of distress

for what's left of you Darkness
in my mouth the clouds are employed
shedding important questions about being

always partially formed I possess nothing
I wouldn't leave in a field or bury in flowers
        to fuck with

the senselessness of completeness in every pattern
putting on my pants or the water
        to boil I want to

point at the glow
it was someone's job to give form to

that others might stand below it feeling
        something new entirely every moment

a ghost undressing itself for a future
where the sky quits being a ceiling and my signature
          quits being my name

there will be a single moment to consider
                    what to give and what
          to give up before

               magnolia

          magnolia

                 magnolia trees

being vicious and green some obscene holy
          difference between what's fully formed
and what's a phone call
               into the abyss just imagine

you are a person with an entire life ahead
          all pain and apricots the sprawl we frame

this rapt imbalance in a voice
          my voice chews on attempting

               to touch the endless
amiable blur we have each given a secret name to

               where under one's wonder attention
sees and seizes this uncertainty what feels
                    like yarn in your chest or how

bells sometimes must be broken
          or turned into bullets
                    I'd defend your lips against
everything but milkshakes my friend she's got

a pretty good hold on being
                some gorgeous thinking
some names carved on a tree convincing me

there's nothing sentimental about axes

we are going to buy all the best sweaters
be a herd of weather asking how much
        more complicated can this get
without becoming a bird
                a bed where we lie

        putting words against a neck that will be
so hard later to describe   the shape of a body
                where Darkness made a home in me

I nested until I had the ocean
        to prove it wrong I wrote

        this light
this letter needs no reply just
                listen my heart

        is cheering

                a little bloody cheer

TODAY I WOKE UP BAFFLED

Today I woke up baffled   The light
questioning everything & everything answering
OK OK I am ready   A shower curtain   A storm
of daffodils continuing to be alive
The whole day a possibly wet thing
full of responsibility   My mouth doesn't want
to play along   It wants some fine noise
I can loosen myself in   It wants that friend
with her way of saying *You are not dead*
just trying   I hook myself to a cup of coffee
to begin again   I mouth & remouth
the word *suddenly* hoping what
happens next will happen   I don't know
if it's a question of being sincere or being true
Though I know when someone says *Suddenly*
it smelled like a field they are being honest
As honest as their body will let them   I can't just stop
using my hands   I can't just walk into the world
& feel fulfilled   I have to try & I have to
want the rain   The rain warm & irreverent
on my skin even if it means nothing   Today
I woke up new & also the same   A horse
without hands   An accident waiting
to happen to everything

A BASIC GUIDE TO SUCCESS

The pair of scissors decides it would like to leave the drawer and become a chainsaw when the pair of scissors visits the museum of natural history it spends hours admiring the saber-toothed cat exhibit for a moment the pair of scissors wants to become a saber-toothed cat when the pair of scissors reads that saber-toothed cats are extinct it leaves the museum later the pair of scissors visits a floral shop where it falls in love with a bouquet of chrysanthemums everyday the pair of scissors cuts its lover's stems shorter and shorter hoping they will live together longer and longer when the chrysanthemums die the pair of scissors grieves by cutting the threads that hold up the clouds the clouds fall onto the earth where the people use chainsaws to take them apart the pair of scissors cuts a door in one of the clouds the people call the door a mouth soon everybody has a mouth

A BASIC GUIDE TO DECISION MAKING

The town decided to build a bridge but they didn't
know what to build it over. The town held a meeting
in the forest to discuss the issue over a PowerPoint
but there wasn't an outlet so the people teamed up
and rubbed their genitals together to generate electricity
and afterwards everyone agreed that the forest was the best
place to rub genitals and they kept rubbing and getting high
until they fell asleep. When the people at the town meeting
woke up they tried to remember the PowerPoint but the past
was like a bleached coral reef and a new town
was established in the forest to celebrate this beginning.
The people from the meeting immediately held a parade.
After a few generations the new town became an old town
and the meaning of the parade became less and less clear, like algebra
or Congress. One year, the parade wandered out of the forest
and discovered an abandoned town no one had ever seen.
In a pile of rubble someone found a Diet Coke. It was
night when the parade returned to the forest and the moon
saturated the town in white pixels. The entire town
woke up to hold a meeting to decide what should be done
with the Diet Coke. It was decided the town would build
a bridge to the place where the Diet Coke had been found.
They did not know why they chose to build a bridge,
only that the idea to build a bridge felt good, just as
rubbing their genitals together felt good. When the bridge
was finished the people from the town would often visit
the other town and hold meetings about different ways to use
Diet Coke and while everyone was talking this one guy
would make origami swans. That guy was the best.

WHAT A TREMENDOUS TIME WE'RE HAVING!

I live in a castle made of ten thousand things
sewn together to make an eye It is a heap
of light It is an adequate castle In the castle
I have made a small version of the world It is
realistic which I know is a mistake There is a pair
of scissors There is a government There are buildings
that break the clouds In the castle I am alive
like a horse My emotions want to make me say things
that will never come back out of you A butterfly
is licking my ear is what my emotions want to say
But the government wants me to tell you things
that do not make sense with my emotions
I have the feeling I am being watched I have
the feeling a flower is going to bite my hand off
The parents & the birds are always quiet
Sometimes I think the castle is not a castle
Other times I lie down in this little world
to make the trees not look like trees

I KEEP FORGETTING THAT EVERYTHING YOU SAY IS CONNECTED

The pamphlet contains no information
regarding how little a bed can be or what
you are doing with those teacups   You with
the what face in the what grass   Who saves who
when information is lacking   The pamphlet
keeps talking about bees & how funny
it is to be an appendage   An actual
canyon   I just keep moving through
towards a very common problem   Everything
divided by something   Like how to know that
something without touching it   Me
& this couch   All those citizens
in the field   Some friends in Tennessee
not fighting a war or anything   Just seeing
a peacock over a lake I feel totally
cardiovascular   How I keep it in
I don't know   In the afterlife I think
I'll be almost the opposite of instructions
Kind of blurry   Wishing I could stay
here or in Tennessee or wherever else
you are   You with the sad face
in the sad grass   More than an appendage
More than a bed   Kind of like a bee
Meaning if you really love something
lick it

A BASIC GUIDE TO SCIENCE

In the abyss, further abysses.
One looks so deep into the abyss
they themselves become an abyss.
The oak tree, an abyss. The dog
whimpering in the snow, an abyss.
The newborn, an abyss created
in a mirror of living abysses. Many
believe the abyss has four chambers
like the heart, that it tastes like copper.
Others are of the opinion the abyss
is definitively abyss-shaped, that it feels
like the darkness inside an egg
though it often sounds like wind chimes.
The abyss wishes to remain anonymous.
The abyss considers itself a close friend,
even when one yells into it, the abyss
does not yell back. The pocket, an abyss.
The stone, an abyss. The throat, an abyss
into which one crawls and calls home.
The abyss the abyss the abyss the abyss
is a window built of tinier windows
made from individual grains of sand.
When one looks through this window
it is as if their eyes are unopened parachutes,
it is as if the abyss were a word, a mist, a wish
rollicking between being and believing.

THREE-SIDED SQUARE

A door is a portal   A painting
is an emotion   Clouds in the diorama
try to mean clouds in the sky   It is clear
the casual vibration of everything against everything
presents us with real errors   In thinking
In feeling   I leave them on a hill
lacking scale or center   In your impossible bed
the proper actions fail me   One thing
always another thing   Ferris wheel
& lemon tree   First kiss & last   Some weird
breed of potential   Like put the emotion
next to the portal   Put the door
in the painting   I can tolerate that   Not knowing
what the shape of this shape is   Though of course
I know somewhere   But by now I'm tilted back
into my face's face   I'm taping pollen
back to the flowers   Just trying to
try harder ends in like like like & I can't
get it right   It's just like that   A video
of me & a camel where I am trying to be
the not-real camel   I'm not kidding
It's a real thing   People kissing
in the kitchen   A need to put the doors
back on their hinges   Or not   To leave
it all open   Not correct   Not anything
other than what it is   So when I say I love you
I'm not wrong   I'm just not in control
Every side of me uncorrected   The best I can do
to make it fit

UPSTAIRS WITH HIS SANDWICH

Instinct to assemble   Instinct to hoping
things will turn out for the better
That's how I got here   With nothing to show
but this fixation on what can't be fixed
Din & contradiction   Shame & splendor
spilling into all the living rooms & dance floors
we've shared   A belief in the ruins
of our own conclusions colludes us into battle
& crumble   Screaming that you mean so much
to meaning   Despite this acre of erratic light
I keep sinking into the same damn things
over & over   In front of all these people
open & worse than ordinary   Another guy
with a sandwich   Another other at the edge
of the awful   I'd be wiser to abandon this
vagueness & go talk to that girl in the green shirt
Ask her where fleeth the wonder   What
kind of flowers I should fill this room with
to have her   Beautiful beautiful   Animal
animal   It's so great we have the capacity
to kiss each other's faces   It's so great
I lost everything   Even my sandwich
Even my exclamation points   Though you know
I'm exaggerating now   I'm miles away   I'm
over there admiring your tomatoes   Glee & grain
alcohol   Happenstance & hopelessness
What I lost wasn't everything

WHAT A TREMENDOUS TIME WE'RE HAVING!

I stand by the armoire & perform experiments
It is technical but not in a very French way
People are always trying to make things
complicated & sometimes that is not so beautiful
like with supercommittees & etiquette I say
fuck it My skin is a delicate golden zoo &
my heart is a ukulele making out with a theremin
It is only beginning to sound right & this is
the purpose of experiments Lay in the grass all day
& it will quietly repair itself in the dark Each blade
industriously licking at next day's dawn
The human part of you will celebrate & that
is what we want To fall asleep in the sun
& wake up with half your body pinned to light

A BASIC GUIDE TO GROWING UP

The birds were surprisingly cordial making nests
in and around our elaborate heads the trees were
in love and no one noticed and no one asked why
our heads were so attractive you had a great ass
and I had a new dress and we were going to the
jubilee but when we woke up it was only the river
dressed in moss and pieces of broken plates and
the clouds needed our help they needed us to
hurry quick to the pharmacy and get the ladder
but the ladder wasn't in the cards and neither was
the eight of spades because there it was in the
spokes of that bicycle but the person riding the
bicycle didn't say hello and you never came back
even without the ladder and I was just standing
there with my lonely head in the river in my dress
getting wetter and wetter which was the saddest
part other than the trees until there weren't any
trees and I got a job and a pizza and went home
to the kids who helped take care of the birds who
by that time had kids of their own

BABY HAMMER

Living is a matter of speaking
more often & adamantly through conch shells
Of knowing sometimes it's best to throw everything
on the floor   To cry through a closed door
& figure it out later   To get rid of
a few things in favor of keeping more
avocados around   Dissonance & donuts
Spontaneous & incompleteness   A great digression
in the form of ten apples on your head
It's silly but what else would you rather be
basking in   Running around like an idiot
for the sake of someone else's happiness
You've got to believe it's worth it
to give up every now & then   How else
to use a see-saw than to laugh at the imbalance
we can't help fuck the whole thing up with
New sounds in the morning   New bar
around the corner   Let's take it all in
until nothing's intact   Or let's cut it short
& love   It's true what we do won't touch
everyone   But we can hit what we don't know
hard enough it hits us back   A little
reverberation   A little book teaching you
what shoes & eyes are   Learn to point
Pick it up & point at yourself   Learn
to say bye bye   Say you never know
how things will turn out   Repeat & repeat
Hit & hit again   There's no reason to cry
until there is & even then   Even aflame
today is going to be a good day

EVERYTHING LOOKS SMALLER TODAY

You say   We are not correctly
alone & that makes me feel
pretty champagne   Gives me animal
focus   Gives me reason to erupt
unregulated bramble   A little
embroidered hooray   Gathered
around the pizza we are inconsolable
with want   It's true   There are enough
silly hats to go around   Enough
basements to fill with volume   But today
I'm lacking the appropriate grace
to be good to this world   I say
the stupidest things   I take a piece
I don't deserve   I set important
things on fire because a cage
is a cage & if I'm to keep living I've got to
dismantle something beautiful   I know
I'm not a worthy man   All I've got
is empathy for a bee   A smile
when your door finally opens   Just
enough pressure   Just enough lukewarm
coffee for both of us   So please outlast me
& forgive me my daily indifference
You've got the wild pony   I've got
this sea   Tonight that's bigger
than both of us   A smaller us
dragging the light back where it belongs

WHAT A TREMENDOUS TIME WE'RE HAVING!

A whale is not a type of information
Neither is a ship's rigging nor a peach tree
If you were not alive you would already
know this When my friends come over
we sit on the carpet & fall into obscurity
because we do not love information
We sit on the pier & watch the water
be ancient fabric We go to the museum
with fresh basil leaves in our pockets
I stand in front of this one Magritte
& shove dreams into my mouth
until my teeth are a kind of bird

A BASIC GUIDE TO FRIENDSHIP

I squeeze the lime into the margarita bucket
the wallpaper has never looked so yellow the
sun is setting and not far away the missiles are
waiting in their missile nests but I am not
worried I have two pounds of margarita and
there are enchiladas in the oven my television
is filled with scientists pounding the
permafrost the internet is warm the cheese is
melted I look out the window for the first
time and notice daffodils I take a big drink of
margarita I look in the mirror in the mirror
the world is covered in different kinds of
death my car needs an oil change the daffodils
kiss the grass it's not up to me the scientists
have found something the phone rings and
it's true it's true you are coming over we are
going to eat these enchiladas

THE NEW PAINT ON MY MANNERS

Full of nothing & bird noise
I'm dancing again   Being completely
undone & that's long overdue
The piano totally sherbet in the bloodstream
A funny mustache   A funny wet
hello in another language   The night
denting me with joy   Forever & ever
I would actually like to be in a tree   Kissing
every leaf on its wild lips   Making useless
gestures in the sun   But oh baby nothing
is useless   Everything is knotted
pretty fantastic   Laced with loneliness
& baby animals & glockenspiels   So I can't
help pick up the phone & call you
Murmur colors at you   Have another
just okay beer & another   Anything
for the kind hush   Whatever isn't
only the middle of how you spell glowing
So let's shoulder up   Put too many people
in a booth & order something that sounds
nicer   Field of familiar hair   A way
to acknowledge our power
over nothing   A nothing to hold onto
Something small & unruly   Overrun
with horses & flames   What's made
for what's dark

WHAT A TREMENDOUS TIME WE'RE HAVING!

My head recently reported it has reached
a resolution to work towards a resolution
I stand in the yard eating pie with my fingers
feeling uncertain about buying
another roll of wrapping paper when
everything is already such a mystery
Trees touching other trees
The morning air against my typeface
I spend all day stranded on this digital archipelago
liking everything My spirit animal is a bear
with a confetti cannon strapped to its back
The point is to surprise you & then maul you
into pieces of joy

NEW LOVE

It's not up to me   It's always
upending me   Leaving me soggy
& grateful & sleeping next to mountains
Soaked in a weird hue of whatever
the flowers need to get by   Ask me
how many times I have to leave
before I'm gone   Ask me what
is in these scones   A little anarchy
& currants never hurt anyone   I'm probably
wrong about that   I've been wrong
for a damn long while now & even
fireflies in the courtyard give me a hope
I can't hide from   Tragedy & ecstasy
& a cup of coffee & the ducks
looking ridiculous just to get by
Me trying to extract the unknowable
from this tiny piano   You on a train
with your questions & smiling   I'm sure
I don't have to tell you what's new
isn't the love   It's the way
you touch the window without caring
you can't stop what passes by   That's it
The rest is shit & glorious
mercy   Ankle in the light   Note
on the windshield   All this brutal
leisure   Let me say it simply   I need you
to help me finish this scone

WILDER BASKETS

All day the eye jumps from one
point of interest to another   The day is
brimming with points of interest   Marvelous
goose in the pond   Me & my sombrero
Swamp I mistake for an airplane   It is
only natural   But what is natural is
all guesswork   Green sweater
abandoned   Field of tiny corn   I see
a spider on a shoe   That is my secret
Asking what isn't art   Like a wedding planner
thawing a box of butterflies   Like
we have so much time to love everything
so don't stop   Repackaging brightness
I think that is our job   To sit in the pines
experiencing strong emotions   Syncing
our sprinkler systems to make us look
delicious   Even when the parachute
that saves you comes down around you
be baffled   Give in & guess   A new kind
of sky   Something you can't escape
reminding you of home   All day
we are lemon-scented   All day
we are ruthless & good   Points of interest
pillow into questions   In a positive light
the answer seems to be   Cherish
what you can   Hold what you can't
together   Elephants huddled in the dark
Your hand on the drawstring   Not sure
what to do next   Just imagine
the answer is yes

I FEEL YES

I climb into the machine and spend
two days thinking about lemonade.
I want to drink lemonade and watch the light
disappear into where I am speaking.
Language enters my life an infection in drag,
my hands feeling plural as if they're hands
but also two or more kinds of vegetables
grown in a country where the sky touches
the distant mountains in a way that is
both beautiful and meaningless, the clouds
heavy static above the village where underwear
dries on a log while a small, ageless girl
stares at the words on a bottle of soda,
not understanding the language though
imagining she does, imagining a vast
world in which this object has meaning or
(which do you think is more important?) value,
imagining the sun cut from the sky and
kept in her pocket next to a smooth cold stone
from the river where her brothers swim
and nothing is digital, and even though
lemonade is unheard of, a state of affairs
that says little about my hands (what is
there to say?), it's good enough and happening
and now here we are and I am glad. I feel
like a birthday is a good reason to be naked.
How about you? What do you think pleasure
smells like? What is your understanding of
the expression *to make one's hackles rise?*
I'm going to say now I'm not in control.
My t-shirt could eat me – it just seems obvious
but either way I'm going to ask you to dance.

We'll make smoothies out of rain and ride
motorcycles through fields of what has to be
commercially-grown lavender, how else
could there be so much of it? I'll tell you
many different things have the ability
to glimmer and that is as much a reason
for joy as for terror. Do you think of what
you eat as having come from a carcass?
Does part of you not believe yourself
when you call it *making love?* Does it sound
like I've been thinking about this for a long time?
I'll never really know anything and that's
why I'm on fire, helping my friend plug a tiny
amplifier into the part of me that still believes
I can wrap my disbelief in birds and bras
and that will be sufficient, or at least loud enough
to dance to without being aware of my body,
which is always in the way because the physical
world is determined by a range of parameters
but what does that matter here? Why not say
everything I feel? Everyday the sun paints me stupid
and I've never been more thankful for anything
than when my skin kisses up to oblivion
in the middle of a parking lot and my
strawberries spill out onto the pavement
like they're alive. Just look at all this! Our heads
more expensive by the minute! I put on a blue coat
and walk into the kingdom. I stand in a puddle
for twenty-five years. I stand in a puddle
and for twenty-five years I am barely born.
Now, stained and weightless, I order Chinese food
in the dark. I watch a video of people
taking off their pants in public. I watch a video
of a video of a lion eating an antelope.
I don't want to understand, I just want

to know you can hear me. My heart is pure
but I didn't say that. I'm just a bastard
cloud confusing the light, a stupid hunk
of ones and zeros trying not to not
foul up the wires. I'm stranded on the edge
of the electorate cooking my hands
in their own juices. I want to be delirious
as a cheerleader full of candy! To express myself
in increasing wolf. I want to rent out
your respiratory system with my airwaves.
Call me a man and I'll fill you with mixtapes
until you dance the feedback out of me.
My actions are excessive! Ice cream in Belarus!
October in a tree! Some precise blur
instructs me. That's how I wrote this,
hovering above the desert in a motionless vessel.
I put a giraffe in a boat and laugh.
Thinking about it isn't going to help.
Somewhere near me my inbox vibrates.
I don't have any business. I feel emotional.
I'm wasting my time. How many ways can I say
something wrong. There's piano skin
on my windowpane! Gravy sticking out of the night!
My multitasking awash in tapestries of light!
Revelation is ubiquitous, McNuggets in the grass.
I'm trying to live better, and many other things.
Every spring the meadow in its hysterical dress
and I all human and delusion. I vow through
the brouhaha with a temple in my fingerprint.
I vow through midnight with a swan
in my bourbon. I vow orgasms and antlers.
I vow to get up. And I do. But who am I
kidding? I'm not in charge. I mimic
the noise of insatiable flowers. I dress up
like a meadow and pretend I'm the world.

When I speak it is the opposite of bones.
Real life bones, my name on my hands.
I understand now, the valley full of brains.
Let's have a conversation using only our skin.
Here I'll start where I'm lonely and wet.
I will never be as good as the snow
breeding in the clouds and the world
eating the snow as it falls around the birds,
the real life birds that are ridiculous tools,
the real life birds that should be arrested
but are not, and the birds in the machine
as it hums and humans and the humming
now a kind of snow that builds and hums,
humming into the world that is a real life bird,
a bird a machine inside a real life word,
a word a totem of inarticulate grammars and grammar
a bird that should be arrested but is not. I just want
to be simple and hanging out a window with my hands
in the sky. To never die, that is the nature of
the machine, the machine that is only fog
between my fingers, the idea of a lake
emerging from the idea of rain, the idea that
I can say something and you will hear it.
That is how I know I am here. Here with birds
and stupidity and pieces of weather. Here where
I drive around all day in the blue light revolving.
Here where I speak in the shape of other humans
speaking. Here where I compare life to an avocado
and the university trembles! I drink lemonade
next to a whale. I drink lemonade and migrate
into a system of becoming. I drink lemonade
and establish relationships based on love
for things that are invisible, or in other words,
faith, which, along with stupidity,
is what brought me here thinking

about lemonade in the first place and
if I had to conceptualize what I mean
by "first place," which is an expression
that denotes a temporal sequence
in terms of an abstracted spatial structure,
the beautiful thing about what I would say
is that I never knew that just thinking
about lemonade would get me here
like how when I pull a bag of oranges
out of a dumpster and make juice from them
and I'm drinking it I think about the person
who works for the grocery store who decided
to throw away that bag of oranges or who
was ordered to throw away that bag of oranges
because of the rotten orange at the bottom
and how when that grocery story employee
absent-mindedly, or perhaps not, perhaps
with a high degree of awareness, tossed
that bag of oranges into the dumpster that
person would never have imagined another person
ever touching those oranges again, let alone
eating them, and then I think back
to the truck that delivered the oranges
and the person who drove that truck and
how they might have touched these oranges
not thinking of them as oranges but as
only some materialized idea of the continual
struggle to understand how to live while
also working and doing something meaningful or
(which do you think is more important?) valuable,
and then I think back to the building
where the oranges were sorted and stickered
and bagged and back to the first truck
that took the oranges from the orange grove
and the people who picked the oranges

with their lives and the things they love and hate
and their thoughts when they read the news
and their lips and bedrooms and hands,
their hands always smelling of oranges,
which may or may not be meaningful or
(which do you think is more important?) valuable,
and their orgasms, shared or not, and how this
incongruous system of human and nonhuman motion
could lead to this bag of oranges in a dumpster
without any mouth to take in their architecture,
without these oranges satisfying some need, some
basic, universal, almost tangible need to know
that our existence is purposeful, which is often
the way one feels sitting on a park bench holding
a single orange barely caring what happens,
and how the breakdown of such a system is
something we all have to account for in our own ways
and how writing this poem feels like that,
confusion coupled with action mixed with some
vague hope that we'll somehow get somewhere,
which is why I climbed into the machine at all.
Then as long as we're here together let's agree
there be no knowing in the making, a knot,
that it show how in the motion, the machinery.
Let's agree that the only thing shared by nations
and snow is that no matter what they touch
they always disappear. Let's agree that if I took
a picture of your face right now and later showed it
to a stranger they would say *Who is this beautiful person
I do not know?* and I would say *I do not know*
because I do not pretend to know you, I only pretend
to speak. And let's agree that in the light
making its way quietly through the valley
there are noises no one knows exist that communicate
nothing and are never repeated and in that light

there is one perpetual question every person
and poem exists to answer, essentially
what's so hard about being happy being
in awe of everything? I need to believe
I would suffer to save you. Amidst cell phones
and bar glass kissing and smashing my face sentimental
for better or for worse or for even better, galloping
full of wine into the parade, removing the plexiglas
between our bodies and our bodies, and our bodies
discovering what they mean when they say
"I am in love with an emergency of symbols!"
What part of a moose don't you understand?
What would it take for you to take off your pants
in public? What if I took off my pants right now
and laid down in the grass, if we could find any,
and in an unsexual way asked you to join me?
Is that even possible? What part of the question
do you think I'm referring to and what do you think
I mean by "possible"? I generate hogwash
in my torso! The proper use of a hammer
is to wear a petticoat and be inconsistent!
A feverish joy scatters into the citizenry!
Isn't this what's supposed to happen
going from meaning to meat to mouth?
The president stands naked in the middle
of the forest! I make sandwiches
for everyone who hates me! After that
what happens is made of fucking flowers.
I look out my window at the light
licking snow off the dumb bodies of air
conditioning units and finally get a grasp
on why everything I love is so leaving.
Why something in a word out of its body
makes me feel everywhere as air, air that lives
in mouths and birds all peach pie and dynamite.

All genetic ballistics in the begonias. I am
the first person ever to touch this tree and for this
the thing that is the word that is my soul
is happy. I mumble into the incredible.
I kiss the idea of peace and give in to feeling
vulnerable to what's foreign about my teeth.
Believe me I swear what I mean when I'm lying.
I want to cuddle until our bodies go
gossamer. I want to know how much gasoline
it would take to get me and all my friends
to California. I want to know what would happen
if instead of gasoline it was lemonade and instead
of California it was the kind of sky that happens
over California and instead of the sky over
California it was just me and you and a bag of oranges
astonishing our faces. It has something to do with
how I want to build a symphony for breakfast. How
I'm angry at clouds. How sometimes I imagine
my credit card laying in the muck at the bottom
of the ocean surrounded by glowing tubes
eating other glowing tubes. How I want to collide
with everything. It takes a wound for a wound
to heal and I need the light to make a mistake of me.
Chemical fantastic, this world inexplicable.
I prop open the screen door with a broken
harmonium. I vote for a lake. I breathe
the same air as birds. I wrap myself in beer.
I was born here of parents born here
from parents the same. They went to work
between boilers and ate tires with Hart Crane.
They walked on their elbows to lick fire
from the river. They got divorces
and more divorces and I got myself a name.
The name a child at the end of its body.
Like in the infant dark an instinctual verb.

A glitch in the organ of my name. My name
displaced from its architecture and there
the machine approaching me like an animal
tamer lonely for its animal and both of us
asleep in some plural center, though
on the periphery my body never sleeps,
since the day I was born – code stumbling
and unclear, an ecosystem inventing itself
under the overpass, and you and me and
all our friends touching our gonads
as if our hands were about to go extinct,
as if I couldn't say at least one thing
that matters even the slightest bit to someone,
as if language is an exit with no way out
and we're all scratching our names into
the final obelisk surrounded by the perfume
of a thousand thousand wires tattooed
to the air emitting tongueless mysteries
in the amphitheatres of our heavy skulls
where some unknowable yawning limit
infects us with the flesh of the entire universe,
airplanes full of wilderness nuzzling the stars,
and a young, ageless girl cutting the sun from the sky
and keeping it in her pocket next to a cold
smooth stone from the river where her brothers
swim and nothing is digital, a young girl
not responsible for the pageant between
her ears and hence imagining no war
other than the tension between the space
where the pattern ends and whatever
isn't the pattern begins. Does it bother you
that in the dark the billboards are still there?
Do you have an understanding of the legal system
of your country in relation to other countries?
Would it be beautiful to be a window?

Would you rather be sincere or a river?
Does camping make you feel less complicit?
Complicit in what? What lobular fervor?
Which ocean of whiskey? Why can't I
stop loving you? Rather than answers,
does the asking of these questions point
towards the essential issue to our being
in the world and communicating which is that
language knows more about the world
than we ever will? Or am I framing this wrong?
Does language know anything or is it just
some kind of technology, an aviary, a field
of scissors? Is it worth it to worry or should
I keep thinking about lemonade?
Aren't they the same breed of wolf?
O endless array of the occasional and scarfs!
Dost thou delight in unsober'd music?
I have a notion to essence! I'm running out
of decisions! A bird lives in a bird's mouth
says the letter I've been writing you
every night for ten thousand years. O collateral
dandelion! A blue coat ringing in the kingdom.
This music is a warning: I'm nothing but stupid.
All this is is a fist full of telephones
filled with the same immense voicemail,
an almost translucent string of sounds
resembling light more than language,
the basic message being: I feel fucking yes.
My heart making out with your heart in the mist
of sprinklers, our hips secret beaches sweet
with nonsense and campfire smoke and an illimitable
unspoken feeling that regardless of this being
a complete mistake it is, in fact, complete,
and amidst the ongoing collapse of laughter
my head fills with something that is not control

in favor of reciting sunflowers on some wet wet
interstate perhaps not so far from here where
this system is neverending sufficiently and I
might fall asleep in your daffodils with a smile
smashed against my face. Can you see me
right now or are we far away from each other?
Do you know where I live or what color
my eyes are? Does that matter to you
or would you rather I act like an author?
I have no idea how I've gotten this far
without saying anything about cats.
Does that make us more or less similar?
Do you want to go up on the roof
of wherever you are and drink lemonade
with me? Do you know how close you are
to birds no matter what you're doing?
O human trying! O American bison!
Squirrels, delicious sleep, my ass! Mistakes!
Let's climb a tree and jump into a pile
of ash berries. Let's use my mother's mouth
as a door into my birthday. Let's eat pie
with our fingers and install confetti cannons
set to go off when a sad person walks by.
Let's kneel in the dirt – what is there to say?
Let's write a poem made entirely of lemonade
and email it to God. Let's undress each other
using birds. When I was nineteen I wrote
the way words look is often more interesting
than how they sound and that is something
I didn't fully grasp until I beheaded an ambulance
and swallowed the siren and since then it's been
inappropriate fabulous in my pleasure hive,
echoes twitching in my teeth, excitement
an inexhaustible ignition, evil violins pawing the sky,
reinventing the word flammable to start again

from ashes, blood bucketing in an approximation
of the circumference of an accident that's left
me blessing the abyss and the see-saw, broken
charming swarm feeling good as a pile of chairs
teetering in the tawny dawn. O vulva toggle
derelict and flickering! Lilacs locked in the pillory!
One day I'm going to die and I'll never again
feel the word tambourine rattle on my tongue
and if you don't think it "makes sense" to wear
corsages made of rain disconnected from the sky,
or to draw perforated lines on each others bodies
and rename our favorite parts after Swedish cities,
or to ride vintage mopeds through fogs of moths,
or to tremble in phone booths and feel the bones
under our faces, or to sit in trees and discuss
the entropy of snow, or to illuminate the city
with accumulation and lack of health insurance,
or to feel hummingbird and uncertainty, our flasks
full of fumbling and lightning, or to invent a machine
whose only function is to articulate the feeling
of sitting in a meadow knowing you are going
to leave the person you thought you loved,
or to never carry an umbrella when it rains
because as far as I know it always rains,
then I recommend a steady diet of fucked-up
hope until the ancient wrong that is really
a flock of disasters in human clothing
reveals itself to you as the harvest of wreckage
and incantation growing in the undergrowth
of everybody's confusion. Do you understand
why any ambiguous desire, i.e. lemonade,
would lead to all this? Why I can describe weeping
as radiant? Why a cage made of syntax and sex
is where my heart lives with its little hands
tangling what I think I'm feeling into a large

audible error? I don't need any proof! Religion
in the feedback – I don't need any proof. Anything
beautiful will save you! Truth is too basic, I want it
baffling and static. Just lie down in the grass
with your soul full of swag. Inconsistent the glitch
I sound in my hoping. Do not expect a delay.
Expect wires kissing. Expect the day to spill electric
from the truncated shrine where our mouths
fumble and spill, where artillery is no longer kept
in the drapery, where each moment inherits
the momentum of brittle and raw arrangements.
The neck leaks louder, each move a mangled
allegiance between etiquette and serration.
Notice how the machine breathes and notice,
now, how close your teeth are to your tongue,
tongue that needs no warrant to magnify
the wound that is the formlessness of thought,
tongue drenched in accidental embroidery
from which the design of the machine splinters
into gesture and voice, is infectious in the fact
that our faces are not abstract, that we are
moving deliciously through our lives surrounded
by an influx of feeling in the blooming
people, the people who are my friends wearing
light on their eyes and lavishing one another
in irregular forms of benevolence in this language
in which I am constantly failing to say how much
I love you. You who wear hats and stumble
against concrete and vagary. Who disrupt
the system with one massive, eternal glass
of lemonade that glows and twists the whole
world art-shaped, the wind turning trees
into tonal blur, a thousand voices pushing
the machine through my veins as my friends
speak and sleep in the rain, umbrella-less

and trying, as the pulp and glint of the system
undergoes alteration with one shard of music
rising up from the golden surface of my friends,
let's get free, let's get free, let's get free and feed
the machine our underwear and our birds
and our hands, all of which are both meaningful
and valuable because meaning and value
are unbearably soldered to the meat
of living, so that we have nothing but happiness
and the machine that eats itself and eats itself
eating itself as we move back into the world
making all these fucking mistakes, then
Neil Young, then lawnmowers atop our graves.
But no matter what the grass will keep growing.
The dictionary will cough up its harmonies.
Love will pour out of phonemes and machines
and I will stand next to you, a glass of lemonade
beside a glass of lemonade, and I hope
by then you and I will finally be friends.

ACKNOWLEDGEMENTS AND THANKS

Enormous thanks to the editors of the following journals where many of these poems first appeared, often in slightly different forms:

Inknode, Aesthetix, Jellyfish, Banango Street, iO: A Journal of New American Poetry, Stoked, Secret Journal, Indigest, Ilk, The Bakery, SCUD, Typo, Red Lightbulbs, Dinosaur Bees, Dark Sky, Forklift, Ohio, jubilat, The New Megaphone, Sixth Finch, Sink, and *Columbia Poetry Review.*

"What a Tremendous Time We're Having!" [All morning I linger in the courtyard] was included in *21 Love Poems: A Cassette Anthology* from Hell Yes Press.

Parts of this book were included in the chapbooks *WHAT A TREMENDOUS TIME WE'RE HAVING!* (iO Books), *A Basic Guide* (Bateau), *Beautiful Out* (H_NGM_N), and *I Feel Yes* (Forklift, Ink). To those editors, my love and thanks.

Endless thanks to my friends and allies, without whom the light wouldn't be worth singing: Wendy Xu, Mike Krutel and Jamie Suvak, Carrie Lorig, Alexis Pope and Justin Crutchley, Joshua Kleinberg, Matt Hart, Nate Pritts, Tyler Gobble and Layne Ransom, Leora Fridman, Caroline Cabrera and Phil Muller, Gale Thompson, Kelin Loe and Michael Gulden, Marc McKee, Daniel Beauregard, Chris Richards, Erica Hoosic, Kory Calico, Bill Devine, Alexis Orgera, Steven Karl, Emily Kendal Frey, Ashley Ford, Ramona Paul, Elaine Hullihen, Nate and Andrea Slawson, Curtis Purdue, Dave Carulli, Stephen Danos, Dolly Lemke, Ryan Spooner, Jeffrey Allen and Holly Amos, Jeff Hipsher, Russ Woods, Michael Goroff, Ted Powers, Mike Wall, Anne Cecilia Holmes, Kyle McCord, Joshua Ware, Noah

Falck, Molly Brodak, Erika Jo Brown and B.J. Love, Joseph and Katie Boldensmith, Bruce Covey, Gina Myers, Aby Sullivan, Maria Varonis and Jimmy Bigley, Tom Kychun, Chad Redden, S.E. Smith, Zac Buck, Matt Guenette, Adam Fell, Thomas Patrick Levy, Chris Smith, Nicki Brown and Patrick Walsh, Christopher Higgs, Katherine Sullivan, Matthew Zapruder, John Gallaher, Tom Dukes, Catherine Wing, David Giffels, Mary Biddinger, the Old Canes, the Cuyahoga Valley National Park, and everyone at The Big Big Mess Reading Series.

Special thanks to Michael Dumanis and Noelle Kocot, and, for their support, to the Northeast Ohio Master of Fine Arts Program and Florida State University.

This book is for my parents and for the mountains.

Nick Sturm is the author of a number of chapbooks including, with Wendy Xu, *I Was Not Even Born* (Coconut) and, with Carrie Lorig, *Nancy and The Dutch* (NAP). He is from Akron, Ohio and lives in Tallahassee, Florida.

LETTUCE

Kevin grows lettuce. Kevin hugs you when you come to talk
about lettuce. He gives you a hug and two handfuls of rain
and all his Stevie Nicks albums because he's moving on but
won't say from what. Kevin grows the lettuce and has faith
in the lettuce and his faith gives you faith and that's why
you hug Kevin. Lonely lettuce, holiday lettuce, sleeping lettuce,
lettuce of god, lettuce of war, the first lettuce to be carried
into space, don't give up lettuce, hanging lettuce, hypoallergenic
lettuce, seedless lettuce, boneless lettuce, lettuce en Español,
John Cage lettuce, Hegelian lettuce no one can decide whether
to agree with or not, wild lettuce, my heart is in Cleveland
lettuce: Kevin grows it all. Kevin has a plan. Basically,
keep growing lettuce. Basically, keep moving until it's called
dancing. When you ask Kevin what he loves most
he looks out over his lettuce fields as if he's discovered
the New World and knows it was an accident and that
is why he loves it. Fresh water lettuce, little black dress
lettuce, plea for clemency lettuce, we all need to hold onto
something lettuce, romaine lettuce, Bibb lettuce, some stars
turn into Earth-sized diamonds when they die lettuce,
the last cookie is yours lettuce, Ramada Inn lettuce, little
yellow flowers at the end of America lettuce, a great hope
in how, in the morning, for a moment, your body barely
belongs to you lettuce. Kevin tells you Googling lettuce
will result in approximately 49,900,000 results. He tells you
we all play our part. He tells you how bad it is for the lettuce
that we talk about art like work and love like economics.
Kevin reaches out without touching you and says *A bouquet*
is also something you can pull from the trash. To create anything is
an act of pleasure. To create anything is to articulate the difference
between a horse with a dusting of snow on its mane and a horse
with a wet mane, which might seem like a trivial distinction

but what we know is determined by the smallest degrees of difference
and what do you really know about horses anyway? Stravinsky,
Jesus, John Candy: they all got close but no one actually gets there.
Kevin is full of these things, these things come out of Kevin
and form tiny bridges between his mouth and the world
painted in what it feels like to devote your life to something
that is mostly water. We should all be so lucky lettuce,
there are no guarantees lettuce, staying up all night
just to prove to one another we're here lettuce, muffled
warmth lettuce, what we are exists not in front of the eye
but behind it lettuce, unwanted screws are to be placed
in the bucket lettuce, just try lettuce and keep it together lettuce,
deer head lettuce, hand dryer lettuce, lettuce lettuce, lettuce
of the Edict of Nantes, lettuce of 2680 BC, lettuce of the lettuce
drawer that holds beer and never lettuce. *Let us* says Kevin
take our lives out into the lettuce where inside everything is a smaller
everything, where our bodies might conjugate back to light,
for we know so little and the roads from here are only for leaving
what's good in us behind. Toothbrush in the trashcan lettuce,
she's gone lettuce, middle of nowhere lettuce, sentimental
mixtape lettuce, passion let us have passion lettuce, it's not easy
lettuce, your turquoise sweater lettuce, boil water just to hear
the sound of the kettle lettuce, the small beautiful things you keep
on the bathroom windowsill lettuce, the world is us kissing
under a sheet lettuce, opera libretto lettuce, unintelligible lettuce,
lettuce beyond forgiveness, lettuce beyond the milk of ambiguity,
complete misunderstanding lettuce, there's still a chance
to spend all afternoon in the sun lettuce, it's time to start
giving a shit lettuce because in these rows of dreams Kevin
is handing you a head of lettuce saying *Your heart does what it can*
not to be heard but someone is listening. Anything in a tank top deserves
to be loved. The clouds have only had names for 200 years. There is
so much still to be done.

4028901R00062

Made in the USA
San Bernardino, CA
28 August 2013